Vincent's Poets

Michael Glover

Vincent's Poets

Michael Glover

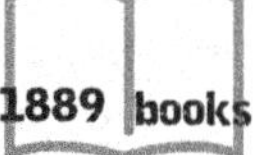

www.1889books.co.uk
ISBN: 978-1-915045-35-5

Other publications by Michael Glover

Poetry :

Measured Lives (1994)
Impossible Horizons (1995)
A Small Modicum of Folly (1997)
The Bead-Eyed Man (1999)
Amidst All This Debris (2001)
For the Sheer Hell of Living (2008)
Only So Much (2011)
Hypothetical May Morning (2018)
Messages to Federico (2018)
What You Do With Days (2019)
One Season in Hell (2020)
The Timely Lift-Off of the Famous Harlequin-Fish (2022)
Mistaking You for a Shower of Summer Confetti (2024)

Others :

Headlong into Pennilessness (2011)
Great Works: Encounters with Art (2016)
Playing Out in the Wireless Days (2017)
111 Places in Sheffield You Shouldn't Miss (2017)
Late Days (2018)
Neo Rauch (2019)
The Book of Extremities (2019)
Thrust (2019)
John Ruskin: an idiosyncratic dictionary (2019)
Rose Wylie (2020)
Whose? (2020)
The Trapper (2021)
Nellie's Devils and Other Stories (2022)
794 Mini Sagas (2023)
The Skittery Zipper (2023)
111 Hidden Art Treasures of London (2024)

As editor or contributor :

Memories of Duveen Brothers (1976)
Goin' down, down, down: Matthew Ronay (2006)
Between Eagles and Pioneers: Georg Baselitz (2011)
Robert Therrien (2016)
Monique Frydman (2017)
A Garland of Poems for Christmas (2022)

Vincent's Poets is published on the occasion of *Van Gogh: Poets and Lovers*, an exhibition staged at The National Gallery, London from 14 September 2024 – 19 January 2025

The quotations are from the letters of Vincent Van Gogh, published online as a free-to-access public resource: vangoghletters.org

Dedication

for Ruth, my strength and stay

It always seems to me that poetry is more sublime than painting; although painting is dirtier, and, when it comes down to it, more annoying. And after all, the painter says nothing; he is silent and I still prefer that.

Extract from letter to Theo Van Gogh
18th September 1888

CONTENTS

The Poet: Portrait of Eugène Boch   2

Portrait of Eugène Boch II   4

The Public Garden Transfigured   6

Vincent's Bedroom   8

Vincent's Chair   9

The Painted Chair   10

The Chair   12

The Endurance of a Chair   13

The Sunflower Speaks   14

The Sunflower Speaks from the Field   16

The Portrait   17

Books! Books! Books!   18

The Artists' Colony   19

Three Strollers   20

Various Recommendations to Gauguin   21

Defiant Morning   22

My Intimate Writers   23

My Pledge to Theo   25

The Muck of Humanity   27

Dante and I   28

Letter to Theo   29

The Demands of a Root   30

Self-Portrait   31

Letting Go   32

Vincent Beyond Reckoning   33

My Dear Familiars   34

Being Never Quite Ready   35

Where is my Muse?   36

A Stroll through the Public Gardens   37

Boccaccio and I   38

Poetry & Painting   39

Running to Meet the World   40

The Offering of Colours   41

The Root's Appeal   42

In the Company of the English   43

The Sunflowers Welcome Me   44

The Companionship of Painting   45

Zola and Flaubert: the Friendship of Story-telling   46

Cypresses   47

The Molten Force of Van Gogh's Sunflowers   48

I'd like to do the portrait of an artist friend who dreams great dreams, who works like the nightingale sings, because that's his nature.

This man will be blond. I'd like to put in the painting my appreciation, my love that I have for him.

I'll paint him, then, just as he is, as faithfully as I can — to begin with.

But that's not how I finish it. To do that, I now become an arbitrary colourist.

I exaggerate the blond of the hair, I come to orange tones, chromes, pale lemon. Behind the head — instead of painting the boring wall of the mean room, I paint the infinite. I make a simple background of the richest, most intense blue that I can prepare, and with this simple combination, the brightly lit blond head, against this rich blue background I get a mysterious effect, like a star in the deep azure.

Extract from letter to Theo
18 August 1888

The Poet: Portrait of Eugène Boch

Something of a poet indeed,
Dantescan perhaps,
All that nerviness to the fore,
A certain tautness, angularity,
The way the head is framed
by that star-lit, daisy-lit sky
Into which he is being absorbed,

And how nature too hangs
In the wheeling firmament,
That depth of ultramarine
He has once again achieved
Into which the eye dives…
How and why Dantescan though?

Borrowing that image
Of an exiled poet in profile,
Red-gowned, a touch ascetic,
The face tapering to the point
Of a goatish, forked, devilish beard,
Cheek bones hollowed,
Brows arched, head bony,

Cut out stark, against the sky,
Eyes intent, watchful,
Brown, to rhyme with
His slope-shouldered, buttoned coat…

A sketch he called it,
Not the real and final thing at all,
Which he made, and then unmade,
Dissatisfied with its finish,
And when he came to send
This sketch to Theo
At Rue Lepic in Paris,

Of the several, it was
The only one framed
And he had called it,
Even sanctified it then, as
The Poet...

Portrait of Eugène Boch II

I have painted that look of infinity in your eyes.
I have given you that this morning,
After the wind dropped,
And the cypresses left off their quivering,
Leaving a strange stillness behind,
Yes, I have sanctified you with it.

The cosmos which wheels behind you
Is the great theatre set
In front of which you,
My Belgian painter of miners
in the Borinage,
Those labouring bodies and souls
Amongst whom I once preached,
Propose yourself today in
Your new identity as The Poet.

You yourself are slowly turning with the stars.
I have stilled you,
Snared you here
For no longer than
the breath of a moment.
What dreams are you dreaming
This morning, my friend?
Where will these stars transport you?

The 'poets' garden' that Vincent can see from his window
at the Yellow House…

*But isn't it true that this garden has a funny sort of style that
means that you can very well imagine the Renaissance poets,
Dante, Petrarch, Boccaccio, strolling among these bushes on the
flowery grass? Now it's true that I've left out some trees, but what
I've kept in the composition is really like that. Only they've
overcrowded it with a number of bushes that aren't in character;
and so to find this truer and more fundamental character, this is
the third time I'm painting the same spot. Now that's the garden
that's right in front of my house, after all.*

Extract from letter to Theo van Gogh,
26th September 1888

The Public Garden Transfigured

Is this as much as it is?
Or as much as it can ever be?
My word against God's?
My brush contending with His?

This tumbled, tousled garden
In all its humdrum simplicity,
As I see it every day,
And now see it again today,

Made new as a hallowed place
For poets and painters to walk in.
I greet them here, just as they greet me,
In mind, memory and fantasy,

Risen up like new made men
To walk with me,
Speaking of such lofty matters
As art, religion and morality.

Did I say mortality?

Van Gogh describes his room in the Yellow House,
aspirationally…

*I want nothing there but straw-bottomed chairs and a table and a
deal bed. The walls whitewashed, the tiles red. But in it I want a
great wealth of portraits and painted studies of figures, which I
plan to do as I go along. I have one to start with, the portrait of
a young Belgian Impressionist; I've painted him as something of a
poet, his refined and nervous head standing out against a deep
ultramarine background of the night sky, with the twinkling of
the stars.*

Extract from letter Willemien Van Gogh
9th and 14th September 1888

Vincent's Bedroom

This is how I want it to be,
With a simple bed,
Two single chairs,
Washbasin, table,
Bare painted boards,
And paintings, many of those,
Around the walls.

Should my sunflowers set off
An almighty blaze
Above it all,
As if bearing in,
With bushels of golden corn,
All the light we could ever need,
Great swags and armfuls of it all,
Brimming and spilling
And even bouncing off the walls?

Oh my sunflowers
Of such golden days as these
Which are yet to come,
When we two will talk
With such fury and abandonment,
Through the long, long
Nights of our colony
Of sweetest amity,
Bathed in all the warmth
And all the light of this
Our most blessed Provence,
Throughout eternity!

Vincent's Chair

I have painted my straw-bottomed chair.
I have stripped it bare.
It is an object of love and attention.
Sit on it – be my guest.
Make yourself as comfortable as you can
As I speak to you of my visions
Now and yet to come.

This chair is all my rootedness.
It goes deep-down into the earth,
With its screw of tobacco, its pipe.
Bathed in morning light,
It invites me to speak true of life,
Not to varnish, aggrandise, or make light…

I shall set it beside his,
At a very particular, skewed angle,
As if we are always
To be seated here together,
Electrifying presences,
Distracted by our endless conversations,
The twists and turns of our tergiversations.
His is a fine made thing
Fresh down from some pedestal,
Mine so plain and humdrum,
Rough worked as I am
And will always be
In my innermost being.

The Painted Chair

Did I say to myself: it must be like this,
Let us begin then, Vincent?
Not at all, it came on, all of a roar,
And all of a rush,
Beyond control of the brush I was wielding,
As it surely always must
Because I am not in control of my gestures.

They run ahead of me like some dog unleashed
From this public garden I can see from my window,
Tousled like all dogs must surely be tousled.
They fling out to left and to right,
Dogs, words, pell-mell out-flingings of the brush,
All of a piece perhaps
With my tempestuous nature,
Always to be so rough-pelted…

And now it is here, hung at a lean on this wall,
Describing back to myself   who else?
Like a busying, hectoring voice
My very own living space.
It says: see the foot-slogging
Ordinariness of you as a man,
Which you surely are, you would tell me,
Unless you would prefer to be a ghost,
Leaning over yourself,
Forever on the wonder and wonder
At the who and the what of
All you have become,

Yes, here you are, Vincent,
All over again, my painterly friend,
As you have so baldly and clumsily signed yourself
On the edge of this box
With its flurry of white onions

By way of public entertainment,
Here you are then, Vincent,
Like some bruised-kneed child
Hailed over to in some schoolyard,
Beaten and battered and
Humdrum as this low chair
You have claimed as your own,
This straw-bottomed chair
For a straw-bottomed being
Such as yourself.

The Chair

This raw, unpainted, left-hand edge,
With multiple nails in-driven,
I regard as a wounding of sorts,
A ripping away of all fatuity, make-believe,
A stabbing down and into the truth of the matter,
And all this surely *does* matter...
See for yourself! It is only a raw webbing
of crude-made, brown-weave canvas after all,
Fit to hang raw in the damp of a midden
Were it not up here on the wall of this bedroom...

In fact, in all this wounding it is myself that I see,
Scarified by all my hauntings,
That which forever must lie beneath
Any smoothness of surface
(Of which there is so pitifully little),
Any garnishings of fine-minted words
Of which, from time to time,
I do seem to have been just about capable...

As I was too, it seems,
Of making this fresh conjured chair
Out of fiercely tamped,
Rough-textured brushstrokes,
Home-spun, four-square
And dependable as these words
Of pitiful description must now
Try to make it, for this is all of me.
Should I then invite you to agree?

The Endurance of a Chair

What could it ever know of the legs
On which it stands, so firm and four-square?
Nothing. It has no powers of reflection.
No chair was ever born a philosopher.

What does it know of its maker,
The man/boy/girl who tapered its legs just so,
Tongued-and-grooved its joints
So that it would all fit together

And bear the strain of some sitter
Such as myself, who will cross his legs
Again and again, like lengths of liquorice
To be twisted and untwisted?

Nothing. It will only ever be this chair
At which I stare when I stare
At its painted portrait on this wall
Because this chair will not outlast me.

It will be burnt and discarded,
As will my body in all its worthlessness.
You will remember us, me and this chair,
Only by this painting in this gallery.

The Sunflower Speaks

1

I have little capacity to express
The nature of the beautiful.
Such words are not in my vocabulary.
I neither vaunt nor self-preen.

I am a serviceable flower,
One amongst thousands in a field,
Blazingly noticeable
Only as one amongst many,

Alongside all my nodding,
Frilly-hat-fringed companions (as you see it),
Lacking the gift of
Heart-stopping singularity,

Lacking the sense or the *politesse*
To woo sozzled air-heads in a sex-stenched room,
Too big and too bruisy to melt
Any light-fingered woman from her pedestal…

Vincent appreciated all of this.
He saw me for what I am.
He knew of my toughness,
He laughed at my mouthy presence.

He watched me tower over you
In contempt for your smallness.
He felt for the fact that I flourish so briefly,
And then shrivel and blacken and harden

To a dense knot of spitty seeds,
Speaking not exactly in anger
(Though do feel free to make that a part of it)
But in pride perhaps

That such a one as I can so
readily beckon to you and to you and to you!

2

Globular and tight,
Crisp, if not nuggety,
Fiercely self-possessed,
Strong in all my armoury,
That is how I would
Describe myself as being.

Pitted, and with a fierce,
Rubbery tenacity,
My stalks, in all their
Tuberose entanglements,
Flowers, my dying bomblets,
Still proudly upstanding.

Never lovely in all this ferocity,
In fact harsh, crude and crusty
With knockabout audacity,
Withering and on the retreat,
Gritty and gravelly.
And all this is why you must love me.

The Sunflower Speaks from the Field

The day job is not at all about beauty.
It is all such a workaday business.
We are a serial being, locked into these fields,
Wave upon wave of us, staring up and out,
Forever sun-thirsty, heavy heads lolling,
Foolish, lop-headed maidens,
Leaning over you as if to woo or to punish…

Vincent has made something of us.
In fact, he claims to define us,
Foolish, manic homunculus that he is.
We shall outlast him.
Our seeds will be scattered over
His grave plot, with telling abandon,
If he does not show caution.

And he never shows caution.
He is always here with us,
Forever wanting things from us,
The true nature of our innermost being, for example,
Or the overarching symbolism of our presence.

It is always such tosh, that together with
His half painted dreams of greatness.
Another errant Dutchman displaced to the balmy South,
Another Dutchman crooning through,
Or perhaps drowning in,
Our fantastical dreams of light everlasting.

The Portrait

This darkness through which I proceed,
It is not the darkness of every day,
It is rather the darkness of me,
In all the rawness and the roughness
Of my inner being.

Would you say that
You had ever truly known me
As I knew myself
On that day you sat in front of me?
I wanted you, always, face forward,
As if nothing else mattered
But the way that you faced me
As if about to interrogate me.

What can you hope to achieve?
You might have asked me.
What do you see here of
All that I am, what can you find
That is not in fact you,
And the meagre fruits
Of your eye, all-seeing?

This is my modernity, your look told me
When I asked it.
What more might we ever need than
A modernity of Vincent's very particular kind,
Ever to haunt futurity?
In short, your look has consumed me.

Books! Books! Books!

Too many words…
Too many books…
Too many to be read…
Such a glut of soul-food
To be greedily absorbed!

When will it arrive,
My latest Zola?
When will I next dive
Into those worlds
which will always strive to define me?

When will I learn what they,
Stacked here at my lonely bedside
(When at last they do arrive),
In their teetering, tottering heaps,
Are here to teach me?

When next will my Shakespeare
Instruct me on the art of nobility,
On what it is to strut and gesture and self-preen
Until the entire world
Has been beaten into submitting
To such greatness?

When will such ease and such greatness be mine?
A cheap edition, of the kind
That I can and will afford,
Must surely soon become available
Thanks to the post-mistress next door.

The Artists' Colony

Having been this old cab horse
From the gloom-struck north
Dragging itself along
Throughout the years of my life,

A new venture has woken me to a fight
That will surely please:
Of painting in the balmy South,
From whence new colours will come,

Bright and various as the companionship
To be found with you and you and you,
My sun-struck, painterly friends,
Standing together as one,

Consumed by talk as bold and electrical
As the sight of these tuberous sunflower stalks
Rising higher than a man's height,
Punching into the sublimity of brash blue skies.

Three Strollers

Botticelli, Petrarch and Dante,
It is these three that I see walking as one
This morning from my window
With the serenity of saints

In my newly, boldly conceived Poets' Garden,
That rag bag of a public park
In front of my gaze,
Transfigured this morning

By sunlight and my own
Furiously beating heart.
What do they speak of, those great ones?
I am not privy to their words.

It is enough for me to know
That they are newly here with me,
Renaissance masters all three,
Connecting me with yet older worlds

Of Latinity, where Virgil praised,
Or blind Homer raged. I shall go over
And snoop on them. How else
Give life to my visions of modernity?

Various Recommendations to Gauguin

Have you read Tartarin, my friend?
Has his friskiness enlivened you?
Or what of Dickens, who recommends
A pipe of an evening
As the perfect antidote for melancholy?

Zola paints his scenes so vividly
That I walk with him, daily.
I know his squalor. I feel for his fury.
Pangloss, on the other hand,
Keeps me afloat with laughter
When I would otherwise drown in misery.

You see, all these are more than friends.
They sustain me through this life.
They have the dependability of
Draughts of good, wholesome wine,
Not the gut-rot stuff from Paris,
On which I barely survived.

Defiant Morning

This morning I rise early again,
And carry my easel into the field,
Attent, feverishly bristling,
To catch it all again,
The light in these parts,
The magnificent, uplifting
Superabundance of it all
In which I drown and I drown
As I drive my legs on,
Morning by morning…

Am I gruff and impatient,
Weaselly of face,
Too short to be noticed?
Is that how you see me?
Do you feel a certain repugnance,
If not defiance, when I stride
Up to your bar, quaff a glass or two
And fling down my cents?
Am I as despicable
As you often believe me to be?

You wait, my madam of madams,
I shall show you something
Of worlds not yet dreamed.
Lop-eared or whole,
I am a part, you will see by and by,
Of all that is yet to be.
They will say: Vincent was here
To make this world real.

My Intimate Writers

These writers of mine, they do things for me
Of a very practical bent –
Take my beloved Dickens, for example.
Had anyone else ever recommended
A pipe of tobacco, a glass of wine,
Bread, and some slivers of cheese

As the best possible remedy against
The soul-freeze that seizes hold
When in contemplation of suicide?
I have tried it, my friend,
And it has worked a treat!
I am soon on the move again,
Easel at the ready,
Out into the fields!

Or let me remind you
Of my many conversations
With my old friend Doctor Pangloss.
Such a cheery fellow!
He too has assured me, times a plenty,
That life must continue
Even as I have stared out
In a mood of unshakeable sullenness and despair
From the windows of this hospital at St Rémy.

Unshakeable? Not at all!
Pangloss has raised me up from this floor
And walked with me as far as the boundary wall
And then out, out into the freedom
Of the to-and-fro swaying of the wheat!

Who else then have I called on in my hours of need?
Oh yes, Ernest Renan above all else perhaps,
He whose command of French,

In his life of Jesus, is like no other's.
It is as if the sound of his words lifts me, bodily,
Up, up into the blueness of the sky,
And then down again, so that I am
Cocking my ear to
The gentle rustling of the olive trees
In the Garden of Gethsemane...
It is not so much history that he gives us
As a species of Resurrection, soul and body...

My Pledge to Theo

This, Theo, is what I must explain to you,
That I have this gulping, compulsive need
To paint the burning reality of my seeing.
It seizes hold of me even as I read
Zola, Balzac, Flaubert and others too
Who are painters in their own right,
Evokers of worlds entire,

Seen, once, at least for me,
(A mere momentary glance,
You could say),
At the corner of a *quai*
In *Bouvard et Pécuchet*,
Or how, in Zola's *L'Assommoir*,
My eyes have followed greedily after
A boulevard stretching away,
That beacon of the new Paris…

My vision is to be made anew, I say it again,
By this venture of the South,
The Poetry of it all, and how it has hereabouts
Long since soaked into the ground,
And this **adv**enture too,
In which the furnishing of my room
In this little house will play a part,

Tipsy walls of no particular distinction
Playing host in time to
A grand decorative scheme
To trumpet my entire being,
Showing off what at last
I might even be capable of in time,
All the diligence I must show
As a pledge of my cast-iron resolution, Theo.

I *always have an animal's coarse appetites. I forget everything for
the external beauty of things, which I'm unable to render because
I make it ugly in my painting, and coarse, whereas nature seems
perfect to me.*

Extract from letter to Paul Gauguin
3rd October 1888

The Muck of Humanity

Being an animal by instinct and appetite,
I make all that I see ugly in the painting.
Coarseness howls to coarseness
Like two mangy dogs across a ravine.

You see, I am an ugly being
With an ugly nature
Who is simply not worthy of
The ravishing perfections of nature.

Unruly too, quick, like a fire, to flare,
Slow to put out, coarse of appetite,
Busy, always, with this dirty and vexing
Business of painting. Pity me in all this making.

Yet is not poetry an even more terrible thing?
Does it not cut to the quick?
Plumb the deepest depths?
I cite Dante, that noble man,

Who passed through Hell
And then on, and up, to Paradise in the end.
Was he not honest, upright, noble?
I, for my part, paint the muck of humanity

As far as I am able.

Dante and I

Dante side on, that is how I see him, always,
The sternness, the austerity, in that beaked nose…
Such nobility, such steadfastness, such resolution
in the steady gaze! He has passed

Through hell, purgatory, and then on,
Until the vision of Beatrice seizes hold,
Lifting him, in Botticelli's marvellous renditions,
To swirl amongst the stars (who are saints),

As if they have now become the lovers
They were never on earth to be…
See how they swim, almost clasping,
At that moment of sheer ecstasy…

Dante's goodness can never be mine
Because I am not a good man.
I am earth-bound, ignoble.
I stride out to the fields, foot slogging….

Yes, it is morning again,
And I am here to confront the world as I always must,
More cart-horse, pulling his heavy load,
Than some saint wafting through the heavens.

Letter to Theo

You must understand, my dear Theo,
That the urgency of the world consumes me.
This is why I am so demanding.
This is why I expect so much from you.

It is not a matter of deserving.
Perhaps I deserve less than nothing.
I write, always, too impetuously.
I ride rough-shod over your feelings.

More paint! More canvases of this size and that!
And as quickly as you can send them!
Is this the entirety of your task then,
To feed my impossible demands upon your good nature?

I am not worthy to be listened to.
And yet ink must flow from this pen
As blood flows. There is no stopping it.
I must do what I must do.

Such fever! Such excess!
Few understand me. Even fewer like me.
You are amongst that precious very few.
And you know that I bless you for it.

Vincent

The Demands of a Root

My dream has found me
In the clasp of a root.
It will not let me go.
It demands to be
Revealed to the world.

I shout: root, root, who are you?
Who gave you such a voice?
Who transported you here
To the bare boards of this room
And invited you into my bed?

It was you! you!, you tell me.
I have no other voice but yours.
It is you who have given this root
That I am some semblance of
The pain of all humanity

Self-Portrait

The face, admittedly, is that of
A rapacious weasel,
As disgusting to myself
As it is to you. No matter.
There is no answer to earthly afflictions

Of the fleshly kind.
God has done what he must do.
Jesus alone is the Creator.
It is he who has twisted
And formed us

Into the scuttling homunculi
Who flood the streets of Paris.
Wine helps a little, of course,
That and the refreshments
To be had at the brothel.

Letting Go

God said: let it all go, all that refinement.
Embrace the coarseness of your inner man.
I let it all go, as he asked. I drifted away.
I bade goodbye to parents, religion, duty,
That desk job of selling paintings
As commodities to sweeten any bourgeois scene.

I painted the miners of the Borinage
Scoffing their feasts of heaped potatoes,
Coarse and real as their appetites.
Millet was with me then.
He and his creed understood my every need.

I went south, for its sunlight.
I dreamt of a colony of artists
Who would understand each other's dreams,
Work in harmony with the rhythms
Of the natural world.
O foolish man that I was and am!

It was the poison of my own character
Which did for me. I understood so little
Of who I am. I resemble a mechanical
Who must career on, on, helpless.
I must be who I must be.
And only death will stop me.

Vincent Beyond Reckoning

Vincent is how I must sign myself.
What more is there to be said?
Is not one name enough for a lifetime?
Do I have to drag forebears behind?

I stand here, skinny, on these bowed legs.
If you saw me, you might turn away.
My breath is a midden at midday,
My singing to be scurried from, at pace!

My father blesses me every day –
When a curse does not better fit the occasion.
What do I know of marriage?
Would I not rather kiss the gutter?

And then, *bam!*, I was dead, self-obliterated,
And there was no more to be said
By me at least. Let your words
Brood and worm around my bones.

I am beyond all your reckonings.

My Dear Familiars

Zola said to me: live life to the full!
Burn it to the embers!
Leave no glass un-drunk!
I toasted him, again and again, reeling through Paris.

Dickens said: when the glooms
Supervene, light a pipe,
And watch its end glow like new life
Through all that dizzying smoke!

I rode with Maupassant, he and I alone,
In an open-top carriage,
Down *les grands boulevards* of Paris.
It was all that we thirsted to consume.

I call all these men my friends.
When I lose their books, I flail, helpless.
Then Pangloss strikes up, cock of a new dawn,
And I spring forth, belly-fires fresh stoked.

Being Never Quite Ready

There are worlds to be made
From the world beyond this window.
It is a matter of unknotting a rope,
Of seeing beyond and behind
What there is to be seen.

Of course, I am not ready,
I shall never quite be ready.
There is too much to be done.
I shall never be practised enough.
My appetites are too voracious.

And yet if I hold back now,
Indolence will consume me.
Those good little ladies will sap me
Of all strength and all will.
The drink will wash over,
As so often in Paris.

There is nothing for it
But to kick open the door
And carry the easel out
Into the fields of new dawn.

When you are not ready,
When you are never fully prepared,
It is then that you must strike.
Fight off the forces of annihilation!

Where is my Muse?

Petrarch has been close by.
I have walked in his footsteps.
I have almost breathed his breath.
He met his muse, Laura, in these parts:
The church of St Claire in Avignon.

Where is the muse I must live to honour?
Why, when I found her,
Did she not answer my call?
Why did my persistence not reward me?
Why did my own family turn against me?

Am I always to be gauche in my dealings,
Coarse in my habits, raving like a child?
Once I owned a god who would pity me.
Then he withdrew from me.
In fact, he betrayed me.

There is only work, work, work left to me.
Let work heave me upright,
Transport me, transfigure the world,
Reveal to me its inner nature.
All this outward man, frankly, disgusts me.

A Stroll through the Public Gardens

Walk in these public gardens with me.
There is such change and changeability.
Elbow aside the man with newspaper outspread,
Standing solid on his two legs....

I see Petrarch now, with his Laura in tow.
They are so deep in conversation
Close to where the oleanders now grow...
I look again and he is gone from me.

I make it all again, as the seasons change.
This is a place of most precious regeneration,
Where the great ones walk, deep in conversation –
Hot-headed Boccaccio, pacing to and fro

As Dante, all nobility, steps back to consider
The nature of our innermost being,
Dante, fresh from his celestial journeyings.
I watch myself then, falling at the feet of The Poet.

Boccaccio and I

Boccaccio, that sensual man,
Has fallen on his back again
Beside the gravel walk
Of this public garden
I can see from the window
Of this house across the street.

I run across to lend him a hand,
Heave him, cursing, to his feet.
He is all gruffness and ribaldry,
As am I at this sunset hour of the day.
As a twosome we pace
To where the little ladies invite
For a little gentle respite…

Later, we drink together in the bar,
And he regales me with the sights
And the sounds of dearest Italy at nights,
Where voices are sweet with melody,
And clowns, everywhere, tumble
At the poor man's feet…

Poetry & Painting

Poetry makes noises in the air,
From the gentle keenings of desire
To the roughest and most heartfelt of bellowings.

Painting, on the other hand,
Proceeds by silence.
It says nothing, merely

Emerging from the hand,
And often quite quickly,
As if no time is to be lost

Because the burdens of this life
Are its consuming passion,
Being so brittle and so short.

The tears of painting are as noiseless
And private as the release of death
In the end may prove to be.

Running to Meet the World

It is out there, the world!
I do not invent it.
It has invented itself.

Not straightforwardly, not by any means.
It has its teases and its tangles,
At which I must work with my fingers

In order to release
All the consuming brilliance
of this my raging actuality…

Are we speaking of miracles then?
What other word could be its equal?
What other word could release

The howling splendour of new dawn's light
On each and every summer morning,
How it coos ands yells and beckons to me

Until I have scarcely the time
To run stumbling out into the fields
With all this messy clutter of brushes,

Canvases, paints and easels?

The Offering of Colours

There are violent colour contrasts
In all these books that I read.
It is how I see them,
How they throw their images
Onto the screen
Of my innermost being.

Take Zola's *Le Rêve*, for example,
How the gold of his embroiderer
Burns itself like sunlight
Across my very seeing.
It is all so akin to
Each fresh day's summer dawn
In its loud trumpetings
Through this window.

All these yellows swim into view,
Some whole, as if cupped
In a proffered bowl,
Others broken into dagger-like slivvers,
Interweaving, intermeshing…
I feel myself so breathless,
So helpless in their presence…

The Root's Appeal

I have no light left within me.
Only the cold stars beckon to me.
Is it to be lifted then,
This, this my futile body?
Is it not too burdened
With the deepest melancholy?

I have no peace left within me.
There is too much corridor-din:
Voices, voices fleeing
Away from me in all their caterwauling.
This is no place for me.
All that remains to me

Is the consoling breath
Of a view from this window
Onto the inner garden
And the outer fields,
Where rooks lazily wheel
Over the bristlings of wheat.

There is a singular root
My eye has just now seized hold of,
Gripping it for dear life.
That root says – I can hear it now –
Paint me, paint me, paint me
In all the pain of my awkward fistiness!
See me as you see yourself!
Do yourself justice, Vincent!
Lift us both up and into the freshness
Of all our singularity!

In the Company of the English

English writers and painters, you ask me?
Yes, they do me some good.
They are the plain and unvarnished boards
Across which I walk, steadily,
Where my jittery heart
Does not miss a beat.

There is something of a
Monday morning about them,
In all their workaday plainness,
If not their unvarnished austerity.
They carry the world to me
Without exaggeration or grandstanding.
I am, in short, at ease in their company.

In the days of my weakness,
Of which there are many,
When feelings buffet me
Like the sudden onset of a raging gale
Across a field of wheat,
I need their friendship and their solidity.
A lighted pipe in the company
Of Dickens and other like-minded souls,
Is as much as I could ever crave.

The Sunflowers Welcome Me

Did you ask me to exchange a word with you?
I could not. I walked on.
I was in too much of a hurry.
Am I then to be condemned
For a disgusting man?

You say you remember me then,
That I reeked of dirt, sweat,
And seldom bathed,
That I was the very model of
Gruffness, surliness and hostility
When spoken to in your shop.

What of that?
What if your look of
Horror and contempt
Displeased me in my turn?
What if I gave you tit for tat?

Am I then to be condemned for drawing back
And hurrying out empty-handed?
These sunflowers in this field,
They do not reel back, shocked.
They are not disgusted
By my presence amongst them,
Heaving my painter's baggage.
I shall make them then
My everyday companions.
I do not need you.

The Companionship of Painting

God does not exchange a word with me.
Once His Presence consumed me,
As He has consumed my Father life-long.
The two of them leant down to me
As if from the Heavens,
And solemnly blessed me.
I felt the warmth of that blessing
For days on end.
It was a great, fresh-stoked fire inside me,
Making me whole,
A singular, blessed part of everything holy.

Now all that has gone from me.
I feel the chill of a profound inner cold.
It is always a Northern winter inside me.
I have been dispossessed of something
That kept all my parts in order.
I have been scattered to distant places,
Where I wander now, forever seeking.
Am I ever to be whole?

Women have betrayed me.
They have failed to answer my call,
To give back ardour for ardour.
How could they not warm to my sincerity?
Why must they shun me?
And why did my family frown so upon me,
Call me the one to be condemned?
Only this painting gives back to me
All that I ask of it.
Only this painting.
By the quality of its silence,
Does not rise up and reprove me.

Zola and Flaubert:
the Friendship of Story-telling

This novel that I am reading,
I regard it as a painted scene
Into which I can enter,
Or as a scene yet to be painted,
And perhaps by me.
                              The fact is that
It sustains me. It uplifts me.
I feel at one with the characters.
I share their dilemmas, their uncertainties.
I see what they see – a certain boulevard in Paris,
Or, at La Villette, that corner of the *quai*…
In short, they speak to me.
We engage in prolonged conversations
About the nature of our common humanity.

And the poets – my Boccaccio, for example,
So roguish, so sensual –
Who painted the lovers of his day.
He brings them alive for me.
I dance and joke with them, one to one,
When the wine flows freely.

Cypresses

They rise from behind the leaning bunchings
Of the bristling armoury
Of the wheat field's pale gold,
Reeling and thrashing when the wind beats,

Behind which thick curdlings of cloud,
Dense and clotty as whipped cream,
Smudged white, grey or palest yellow,
Fuss and flurry… And still, in spite of all,

They stand tall in the almighty,
Heaven-yearning strain
Of their tapering up-reach,
Spiralling, ever spiralling.

I lose myself in them.
I would, if I could, twist upwards with them.
I call them my ancient of days,
My Egyptian obelisks.

The Molten Force of Van Gogh's Sunflowers

'I, indeed, before others, have taken the sunflower,' wrote Vincent Van Gogh to Paul Gauguin on 21 January 1889 with remarkable assurance for a man of such febrile temperament. Ever since, the whole world has inclined to agree with him. The name Van Gogh has become identified with his various painted representations of it. Without the sunflower there could be no Van Gogh. Without Van Gogh there is no such thing as painted sunflowers.

There were not one, of course, but many. The five most celebrated, all contained within rude vases, are dispersed in museums throughout the world: London, Philadelphia, Munich, Tokyo and Amsterdam, in the Van Gogh Museum.

The version in Amsterdam was painted just a few months after the variation you can see on display at the National Gallery in London. It has been subjected to prolonged scrutiny at the hands of researchers and conservators for two reasons. Such is the global fascination with Van Gogh and his sunflowers – he is art's rock star; the average age of the visitor to the Van Gogh Museum in Amsterdam is 26 – that we are desperate to peer behind the arras. What are its secrets? How was it made? And how has it stood the test of time?

The good news is that the painting is in a pretty good state for its age (130), but it is also a little too fragile to do any more travelling. You'll never see it anywhere other than in Amsterdam. Conservators have also discovered a few useful and fascinating things about its condition. Van Gogh added a strip of wood to the top of the painting to give the sunflowers a little more breathing space.

What is more, the various layers of varnish that were added by ignorant experts over the years, giving the painted surface an unpleasant sheen, were never of Van Gogh's making. He would have hated the way they cause the textured surface of the flower heads to wink back at you when they catch the light. Unfortunately, the varnish has started to merge with the paint, so it is irremovable.

Flower painting was very popular in nineteenth-century France. Flowers were cheap to buy. Flowers paintings sold well. Those are two compelling reasons why Van Gogh might have wanted to add this skill to his repertoire.

But his relationship with sunflowers is something very special, as he well began to understand as he persisted in painting them year on year. These are not flower paintings of a traditional kind at all. They are not pretty adjuncts to a room. Van Gogh's sunflowers are not really decorative at all, as we recognise the more we stand and stare and stare at the one in the National Gallery

Sunflowers are tough-minded, helio-centric, minatory, alarmingly large and robust. Travel along those little lanes between the fields of the Midi, and you will not be able to mistake their character. They weren't everywhere in Van Gogh's day. They are now though.

Van Gogh's sunflowers look like emotional turbulence and unruliness barely contained. They are spiky, dense, tactile, bristly, awkwardly twisty, molten-solid. Each head could be a nasty packed boxing glove. The head looks even more lugubrious in death. Van Gogh's sunflower is a species of self-portraiture, not pretty, not decorative, and certainly not polite. No wonder he was such a torment to himself and others.

MG

Printed in the USA
CPSIA information can be obtained
at www.ICGtesting.com
CBHW052054080924
14022CB00005B/96